# 1·2·3
# I Can Paint!

## Irene Luxbacher

KIDS CAN PRESS

A painting is a **PICTURE** you make with paints.
It can look like something real or something you imagine.
Let's paint places …

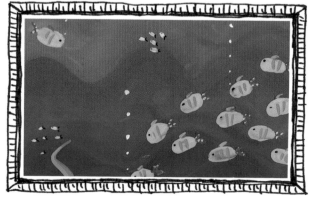

3

The things you use to make a painting are called

# MATERIALS.

• CRAFT PAPER

• OLD NEWSPAPERS (TO PROTECT YOUR WORK SPACE FROM PAINT SPOTS AND SPILLS)

• SMOCK (TO PROTECT YOUR CLOTHES FROM PAINT SPOTS AND SPILLS)

• PLASTIC CONTAINERS OR ALUMINUM PIE PLATES (FOR MIXING YOUR PAINT)

• LIQUID TEMPERA PAINTS OR ACRYLIC PAINTS

4

• BIG AND SMALL PAINTBRUSHES

• TOOTHBRUSH

• BIG AND SMALL SPONGES

• COTTON SWABS

• SCRAPS OF
CARDBOARD

• SMALL FOAM
PAINT ROLLER

# ARTIST SECRET:

Mixing water into thick or goopy paints will help you spread them smoothly over your paper. Add only a little water at a time, though. Too much will make your paint too drippy to paint with.

# MIX It UP

All you need is BLUE, YELLOW and RED paint to mix up an ocean of colors. Dive in and see!

**1.** Drop big blobs of blue paint in the center of your paper. (If you are using finger-painting paper, make sure it is shiny side up.) Spread the paint all around with your fingers. Try to fill up your whole page with lots of wet paint.

**2.** Drop a small blob of yellow paint near the top of your paper. Mix it into some of the wet blue paint. What a beautiful ocean green you've made!

**3.** Drop a small blob of red paint near the bottom of your paper. Mix it into some of the wet blue paint. Now the bottom of your ocean is a deep dark purple.

# SPLASH!
## An Underwater World!

While your painting dries, mix some red and yellow paint together to make orange. Dip your thumb into the paint and press it onto your painting. Keep going until you have a whole school of thumbprint fish. Use a small paintbrush or cotton swab to add colorful fins, tails, stripes and spots to your fish. Now … what else lives in your underwater world?

Blue, yellow and red are called **PRIMARY** colors. When you mix them, they make the **SECONDARY** colors green, orange and purple.

BLUE + YELLOW

= GREEN

RED + YELLOW

= ORANGE

BLUE + RED

= PURPLE

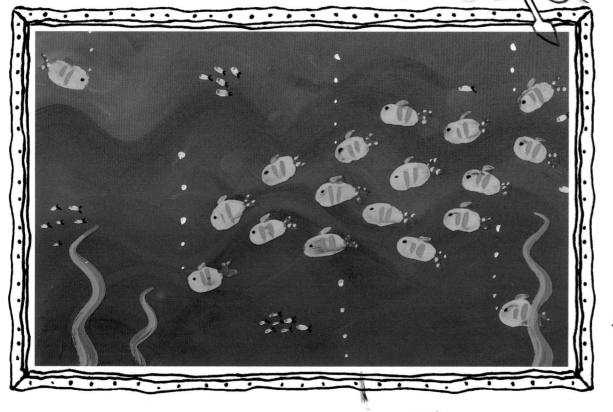

# LIGHT and DARK

What happens when you mix a bit of **WHITE** paint into some green paint? What about when you mix a bit of **BLACK** into green? You can find out by painting a farmer's grassy field.

**1.** Use a foam roller or fat paintbrush to cover your paper with green paint. This is the **BACKGROUND** (the color the rest of the painting is painted on). Let your background dry.

**2.** Mix together a little white paint and a big blob of green paint to make a lighter green. Use your roller or brush to paint a few squares on your background.

**3.** Mix together a tiny bit of black paint and a big blob of green paint to make a darker green. Paint a few dark green rectangles. Let your painting dry.

# WOW!
## A beautiful bird's-eye view!

Imagine you're a bird flying over a farmer's field. What would you see? Dip a small paintbrush in brown paint to add dirt roads. Use the tip of your finger or a sponge to paint colorful little houses and farms — and whatever else a bird's eye might spy.

Every color can be lightened by mixing it with a little white paint or darkened by mixing it with a little black paint. The new colors are TONES of the first color.

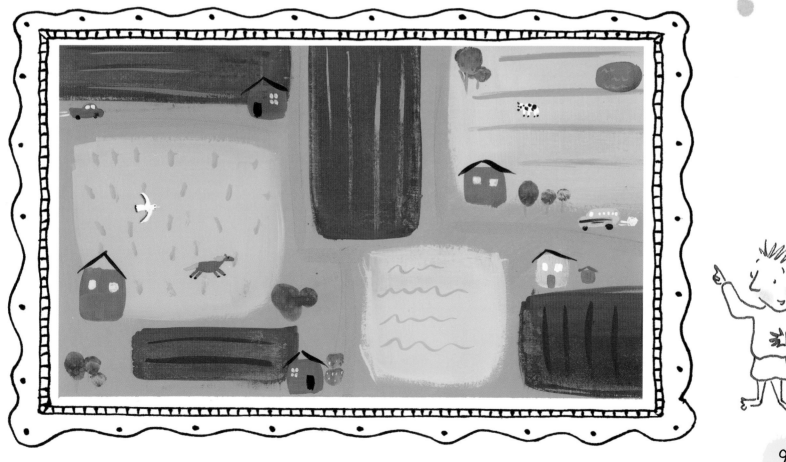

# WARM and FRIENDLY

Have you ever noticed how some colors seem as warm as the sun? Colors such as YELLOW, RED and ORANGE will make your painting of a field of flowers look warm and friendly.

**1.** Mix together a big blob of yellow, a little bit of red and a little bit of brown paint to make a warm orange color. Use a big sponge to cover your paper with an orange background. Let your background dry.

**2.** Use a small sponge to press lots of dark brown spots all over the background. These will be the centers of your flowers. Let the paint dry.

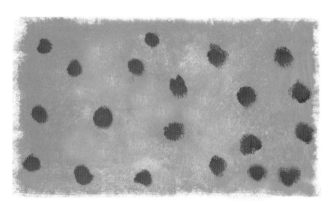

**3.** Mix one blob of yellow with a bit of white paint to make a light yellow. Mix another blob of yellow with a bit of brown or orange for a darker yellow. Use a small paintbrush to paint small lines and dots around each flower center to make flower petals that are different shades of yellow.

# Mmmm ...
## A Sunny Field of Flowers!

Paint a strip of light, bright blue sky across the very top of your flowery field with a big paintbrush. Use a small brush or cotton swab to add green stems and leaves. Is your field of flowers home to colorful insects, too? Use a very small brush or cotton swab to add small dots of color for red ladybugs, yellow bumblebees, green grasshoppers and black spiders.

The colors red, yellow and orange are **WARM COLORS** because they remind us of the sun.

Green, blue and purple are **COOL COLORS** because they remind us of things like grass, water and ice.

# BUSY and BRIGHT

When some colors are painted next to each other, they look like they're ready to jump right off the paper. Painting blue next to orange, red next to green and purple next to yellow will make your painting of a busy city street look BRIGHT and LIVELY.

**1.** Mix a tiny drop of black with a blob of white to make light gray paint. Cover the paper completely to make a background that looks like a gray sky. Let your background dry.

**2.** Use a spoon to drop wet blobs of blue and orange close to each other on part of the background. Next drop blobs of red and green close to each other. Then drop blobs of purple and yellow close to each other.

**3.** Press a square piece of cardboard on one blob of paint and drag it down to the bottom of the paper. Keep doing this until you have a whole city full of buildings and skyscrapers. (Your buildings might touch each other, and that's okay.)

# BEEP BEEP!
## Busy City Streets!

There is so much to see in a busy city! Paint some streets and sidewalks using a fat paintbrush and gray and black paint. Use a small sponge or cotton swab to fill your painting with lots of bright spots of color that look like cars, people and even an airplane flying by! What about painting windows on the buildings, too?

Pairs of colors like blue and orange, green and red or purple and yellow are called COMPLEMENTARY COLORS. They look extra bright and busy beside each other.

# TOUCHING the SKY

Have you ever watched the sun set? What colors do you see in the sky? Think about it while you make this painting of an evening sky over some mountains.

**1.** Use a big paintbrush to cover your paper with a purple background. Let your background dry.

**2.** Mix together a little white paint and a blob of purple paint to make light purple. Use a big paintbrush to paint the light purple evening sky. Start at the top and work your way down, brushing from one edge of the paper to the other. Make sure you leave a strip of the dark purple background across the bottom.

**3.** While the paint is still wet, use a damp sponge or paper towel to rub triangle-shaped mountains along the line where your light purple sky and dark purple background meet.

# LOOK!
## A Full Moon Rising!

Use a very small brush to paint tiny, faraway trees on the sides of your mountains. Use a medium-sized brush to paint bigger, closer trees near the bottom of the paper. Add a blue, winding river that starts out wide at the bottom of the paper and ends in a skinny point at the horizon line. Use a sponge and white paint to dab fluffy clouds and a full moon starting to rise above your purple mountain range.

The line where the ground and sky meet is called the HORIZON LINE.

15

# POWER Painting

Drip, drop, splat! Have fun with your paint and make a night sky *EXPLODING* with colorful *FIREWORKS*.

**1.** Use a big paintbrush to paint your paper completely black to make a night sky background. Let your background dry.

**2.** Cover the bottom of your paper with strips of masking tape. Don't press too hard because you'll need to peel it off later.

**3.** Use a paintbrush, toothbrush and even your fingers to brush, flick and splatter the night sky full of your favorite colors. Let the paint dry and carefully peel the tape off.

# POW!
## Fantastic Fireworks!

Paint little houses and tiny people along the bottom of your paper using a cotton swab or a small paintbrush. Add stars to your night sky by dabbing thick dots of paint onto your picture with a small brush. You can use the tip of your brush handle to scratch star shapes into the wet paint dots.

The way paint is added to a picture is called the TECHNIQUE.

BRUSHING, FLICKING, SPLATTERING and SCRATCHING are all painting techniques.

17

# A WHOLE WIDE WORLD

What would you make if you put all your painted places together in one big painting?
Tape a few pieces of paper together and get ready to paint a **MURAL** of a whole wide world.

### OCEAN

Use a big paintbrush or your fingers to paint a big, deep ocean. Remember that you can mix a little yellow paint with a blob of blue to make an ocean green, and you can mix a little red with a blob of blue to make a deep purple. Let your ocean dry.

### LAND

Use a foam roller or a fat brush to paint green patches of grassy land. Make different tones of green by adding a little white and a little black to your green paint. Let your land dry.

### SKY

Mix a small drop of white paint and a blob of blue. Use a fat brush to paint a blue sky all the way down to the horizon. You can paint a bright yellow sun or add orange and red to your sky if you want it to look like the sun is setting. Let your painted sky dry.

## WARM AND COLD PLACES

Use a sponge to press on spots of yellow, orange and red to paint the parts of your world that are warm and sunny. Use another sponge to press on dots of white, blue and purple to paint the parts of your world that are cold and snowy. Let your warm and cold places dry.

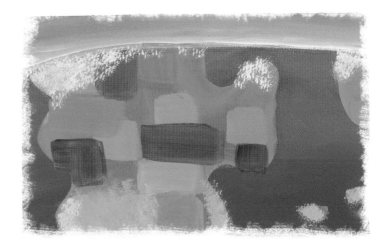

## CITIES

Use a square piece of cardboard to press and drag a few colorful blobs of paint to make the tall buildings of a busy city. Remember, putting together colors like blue and orange, red and green or purple and yellow makes them really stand out. Let your city dry.

## FINISHING TOUCHES

What else do you imagine in your world? If parts of your painting are still wet, you can use a damp sponge or paper towel to rub in some mountains. Use a cotton swab or small sponge to paint colorful little houses, cars or trees. Use a toothbrush to splat and flick spots in the sky that look like faraway birds or stars. Use a small brush to paint flowing rivers, lakes, trees and flowers.

# Out of this WORLD!

Use a small paintbrush and lots of colors to paint some silly people, wild-looking animals and neat creatures that live in your world.

A **MURAL** is a very large painting. It can cover the wall of a room or even the wall of a building!

21

# Note to PARENTS and TEACHERS

We chose scenery as a fun theme for exploring some basic painting techniques, but there are lots of other topics or themes you can use to inspire your young artist. Here are a few ideas to get you started.

• Paint a buffet of your favorite foods. Start with primary colors to paint bright blueberries, red tomatoes or yellow bananas. Now, paint in some more tasty treats by mixing up some secondary colors (see Mix It Up, page 6). And just imagine a festive birthday cake made with dragged, flicked and sprayed paint (see Power Painting, page 16)!

• Or create a farm full of animals. Patches of lightened and darkened paint (see Light and Dark, page 8) can look like the spots on a cow or horse! Try using complementary colors (see Busy and Bright, page 12) to paint bright feathers on a crowing rooster.

Tips to ensure a GOOD PAINTING EXPERIENCE every time:

1. Use inexpensive materials and make sure your young artist's clothes and the work area are protected from spills. This way it's all about the fun, not the waste or the mess.

2. Focus on the process rather than the end product. Make sure your young artist is relaxed and having fun with the information instead of expecting perfection every time.

3. Remind your young artist that mistakes are an artist's best friend. The most interesting painting techniques or color combinations are often discovered by mistake.

# ART Words

### BACKGROUND
page 8

### HORIZON LINE
page 15

### MURAL
page 21

### TECHNIQUES
page 17

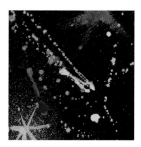

### COMPLEMENTARY COLORS
page 13

### MATERIALS
page 4

### PRIMARY COLORS
page 7

### TONES
page 9

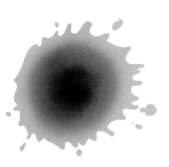

### COOL COLORS
page 11

### SECONDARY COLORS
page 7

### WARM COLORS
page 11

23

FOR MY FAMILY: FRANK, SOPHIA, NICK, LESLIE AND ELIJAH

*Many thanks to Valerie Hussey for her encouragement, and special thanks to Stacey Roderick and Karen Powers for their amazing talents and insights on this project.*

Kids Can Press acknowledges the financial support of the Government of Ontario, through the Ontario Media Development Corporation's Ontario Book Initiative, and the Government of Canada, through the BPIDP, for our publishing activity.

Published in Canada by
Kids Can Press Ltd.
29 Birch Avenue
Toronto, ON  M4V 1E2

Published in the U.S. by
Kids Can Press Ltd.
2250 Military Road
Tonawanda, NY  14150

www.kidscanpress.com

Edited by Stacey Roderick
Designed by Karen Powers
Printed and bound in Singapore

The hardcover edition of this book is smyth sewn casebound.
The paperback edition of this book is limp sewn with a drawn-on cover.

CM 07  0 9 8 7 6 5 4 3 2 1
CM PA 07  0 9 8 7 6 5 4 3 2 1

**Library and Archives Canada Cataloguing in Publication**

Luxbacher, Irene, 1970–
     123 I can paint / written and illustrated by
Irene Luxbacher.

(Starting art)
ISBN 978-1-55453-037-3 (bound)
ISBN 978-1-55453-150-9 (pbk.)

1. Painting—Technique—Juvenile literature.  I. Title.
II. Title: One, two, three I can paint. III.  Series:
Luxbacher, Irene, 1970–   Starting art.

ND1146.L82 2007     j751.4     C2007-900053-3

Kids Can Press is a Corus™ Entertainment company